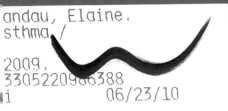
ASTHMA

ELAINE LANDAU

mc Marshall Cavendish
Benchmark
New York

Marshall Cavendish Benchmark
99 White Plains Road
Tarrytown, New York 10591
www.marshallcavendish.us

Expert Reader: Leslie L. Barton, M.D., professor of Pediatrics, University of Arizona College of Medicine, Tucson, Arizona

Library of Congress Cataloging-in-Publication Data
Landau, Elaine.
   Asthma / by Elaine Landau.
      p. cm. — (Head-to-toe health)
   Summary: "Provides basic information about asthma and its prevention"—Provided by publisher.
   Includes bibliographical references and index.
   ISBN 978-0-7614-2845-9
1. Asthma—Juvenile literature. I. Title.

RC591.L32 2009
616.2'38—dc22
2007034998

Editor: Christine Florie
Publisher: Michelle Bisson
Art Director: Anahid Hamparian
Series Designer: Alex Ferrari

Photo research by Connie Gardner

Cover photo by Stockbyte/Getty Images

The photographs in this book are used by permission and through the courtesy of:
Photo Researchers: Lawrence Migdale, 4, 15; Michele S. Graham, 6; David Mack, 9; Eye of Science, 10; Damien Lovegrove, 21; *Super Stock:* age footstock, 7, 16; *Corbis:* Liu Liqun, 10; *Getty Images:* Taxi, 12; Julie Toy, 22; Alistair Berg, 25; *The Image Works:* John Birdsall, 19.

Printed in China
1 3 5 6 4 2

CONTENTS

It's Asthma

It's a cool, crisp fall day. You're on the soccer field with your teammates. Your best friend Danny has the ball. He's running across the field with it. Seconds later he scores a goal!

Everyone cheers. Then, all of sudden, Danny doesn't look very well. He's coughing and **wheezing**. He seems short of breath. The coach sees Danny and takes him over to the sidelines. He can help him there.

Danny's team members know what's happening. Two other boys on the team have been through it themselves. Danny has **asthma**. He is having an **asthma attack**.

WHAT IS ASTHMA ANYWAY?

Asthma is a condition that affects your breathing. The trouble starts in the **airways**. Those are the tubes that bring air in and out of your lungs. When you have asthma the inner walls

◀ An asthma attack can come on when you are most active.

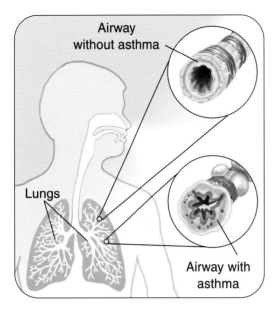

Airway without asthma

Lungs

Airway with asthma

This diagram illustrates airways with and without asthma.

of these tubes become **inflamed** or swollen. During an asthma attack the tubes become even narrower.

Not all asthma attacks are alike. Some can be worse than others. In a very bad attack your airways close up quite a bit. Like Danny, you find it hard to breathe. You may cough or wheeze. There may also be a tight feeling in your chest. One boy described it this way, "I feel like I'm fighting with some unknown force for each breath. Sometimes, I feel like the air comes into my mouth, but will not go down into my lung."

An asthma attack can look and feel scary. That's the bad news. But there's some good news, too. Having asthma does not have to keep you on the sidelines. Although asthma cannot be cured, it can be controlled with proper treatment. Today, many athletes, such as NBA star Dennis Rodman and Olympic medal winner Misty Hyman, have asthma. They do well in all sorts of sports. That includes scoring goals on the soccer field!

GET GOING

Being active can sometimes bring on an
asthma attack. Doctors aren't sure why. Some think that
breathing through your mouth may irritate your airways. If you are
outdoors sometimes air pollution worsens things.
So, if you have asthma, is it best not to take gym or play sports?
Oh, no—get out and go! Everyone needs to be fit and active,
including people with asthma. You can keep your asthma
under control and have a ball—playing ball!

ALL ABOUT ASTHMA

Scientists are not sure what causes asthma. It may be caused by a combination of things. One of these is your family history. If someone in your family has asthma, you are more likely to have it, too.

Asthma attacks are also brought on by different **triggers** in the environment. Among the most common ones are allergies. Not everyone who has allergies has asthma. Yet most people with asthma also have allergies.

Being allergic to animal **dander** has been known to trigger asthma attacks. So, if you're allergic to dogs or cats, please don't pet the pet! Many people with asthma are also allergic to cockroaches. No one needs to be told not to pet those!

Pollen, the tiny grains produced by flowering plants, can be a problem, too. Lots of people are allergic to pollen. It has also been known to trigger asthma attacks.

The blue and green particles in this illustration are common allergens in the lungs. They can trigger an asthma attack.

OH, YUCK! THEY'RE HERE, THERE, AND EVERYWHERE

What is oval, cream-colored,
and has eight feet with sticky pads on the bottom?
If you said dust mites, you are right. Dust mites are too small to see
with the naked eye. Yet they are on your clothing, carpeting, and bedding.
An egg-laying female can produce about ten new dust mites a week.
Dust mites are a common trigger for people with asthma.

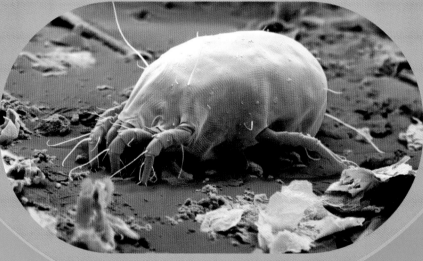

Lastly, allergies to dust are not uncommon. If you have asthma, dust mites are not your friends. These tiny creepy creatures can trigger asthma attacks. Dust is hard to avoid. But if you have asthma, try to stay out of very dusty places.

Other asthma triggers are **irritants**. An irritant can be anything that irritates the lungs' airways. These include cigarette smoke, smoke from a fireplace, air pollution, and strong smells

Irritants in the air, such as pollution, trigger some asthma attacks.

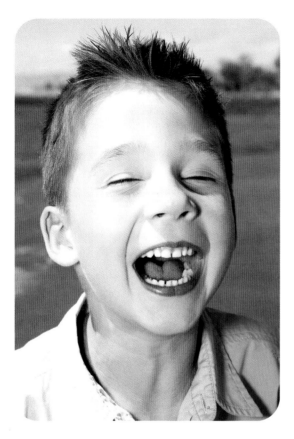

Did somebody just tell this boy a funny joke? Kids with asthma should not think they are going to have an attack whenever they laugh.

like perfume or paint. If you have asthma you don't want to be in a car with someone puffing away on a cigarette. It isn't healthy for you. Smoking isn't good for the smoker either!

At times, changes in the weather can bring on asthma attacks. Crisp, cool weather has been known to trigger them. So has expressing strong emotions. Laughing or crying hard can cause an asthma attack. Yelling can, too. When people express strong emotions, their breathing changes. This doesn't mean that people who have asthma should act like robots. It's important for everyone to show their feelings. Just don't overdo it.

Having a cold, virus, or the flu is unpleasant for anyone. Yet, for people with asthma, some illnesses and infections are even more troublesome. They can trigger attacks. Certain medicines act as triggers as well.

DIFFERENT TRIGGERS AFFECT DIFFERENT FOLKS

There are many other asthma triggers. Not all people with asthma are alike. Something can be a trigger for one person, but not for another.

If you have asthma you need to learn what your triggers are. Your doctor can help you find this out. Then you can work on finding ways to avoid them.

SEEING THE DOCTOR

Think you might have asthma? You need to see a doctor to find out for sure. During your visit, the doctor will ask lots of questions. The doctor needs to know if you have had some of the most common **symptoms**. These are:

- coughing
- wheezing
- shortness of breath
- tightness in chest

The doctor will also ask about your family history.

Usually there will be some tests as well. These check how well your lungs are working. In addition, you may need to take some allergy tests and have a chest X-ray. The doctor has to rule out other conditions. This is important. At times, people with allergies have some of the same symptoms as asthma. Before you can be treated for asthma, a doctor must be sure that you really have asthma.

It is very important to see a doctor if you think you have asthma.

A doctor will give you a plan to follow to help keep your asthma under control.

TREATING ASTHMA

What if you have asthma? Next, the doctor will need to find out how bad your asthma is. This is important in picking the right medicine for you. It will also help the doctor come up with a special plan for you. This plan is called an asthma action plan. An asthma action plan is a handy tool. It will note what will trigger your asthma attack.

Your asthma action plan will also tell you what to do when you start to have symptoms. Your school should have a copy of your plan. So should anyone else who takes care of you. Following the plan will help you control your asthma.

DID YOU KNOW?

Did you know that asthma is the number one reason why kids are absent from school? Young people miss more than fourteen million school days every year due to asthma.

Managing Asthma

Controlling asthma becomes easier with a plan. Since each person is different, each self-management plan is different, too.

Your plan will list your asthma triggers. This will help you know what to try to stay away from.

WHAT TO TAKE AND WHEN TO TAKE IT

The plan will also list the medicines you'll need. People with asthma need two types of medicines: quick relief and long-term.

Quick relief is your emergency relief medicine. You don't take it everyday. You usually only use it when you feel an asthma attack coming on. This medicine works to relax the tightened muscles around your airways. This allows the airways to open more fully.

Quick relief drugs work immediately. You'll feel better right away. These medicines are used with an **inhaler**. An inhaler is

Medicine in an inhaler relieves asthma very quickly.

a small device that lets you inhale medicine through your mouth. Always keep your inhaler with you in case of an attack.

AN INHALER CAN BE YOUR BEST FRIEND

Learn to use your inhaler properly. Your doctor or a nurse at your doctor's office or clinic can show you how to do this. Inhaled medicines are ideal for people with asthma. The medicine goes straight to the lungs—just where you need it.

Long-term medicine must be taken daily. It works to reduce the swelling in your airways. This means you'll have fewer asthma attacks. Even if you feel fine, it's important to take your long-term asthma medicine. It will help keep you feeling fine.

USING A PEAK FLOW METER

Many people with asthma have a **peak flow meter** at home. This is a small device that you can hold in your hand. It measures how well your lungs are working.

The peak flow meter is easy to use. First you take in a deep breath. Then you blow the air out into the meter. The meter will give you a number reading. That number shows you how fast the air came out. The higher the number, the easier you are breathing.

The peak flow meter can alert you to early changes in your condition. It can warn you of a possible attack even before you begin to feel the symptoms.

A peak flow meter measures the lung capacity of this girl.

LIVING RIGHT

There are still other things you can do. Taking good care of yourself can help if you have asthma. It's a good idea to try to stay fit. That means eating right and getting enough exercise.

Yoga is an exercise that relaxes the body and helps regulate breathing.

Swimming is an especially good exercise for people with asthma. While you're in a swimming pool, you breathe in warm, moist air. That makes swimming less likely to trigger an asthma attack than some other sports.

Yoga is another great form of exercise if you have asthma. It relaxes your body. Yoga can also help with breathing. People with asthma can enjoy many other sports and types of exercise as well.

Also remember to drink plenty of water. This is especially important when you exercise or have a cold. That's when you tend to lose fluids. It's important to replace these.

Lastly, be careful when taking your medicines. Be sure to take your daily medicine every day. Try not to overuse the medicine you take for quick relief. Only reach for it when you really need it.

You can learn to manage your asthma. Having a healthy lifestyle is a step in the right direction.

LIVING WITH ASTHMA

If you have asthma you are not alone. Close to 20 million people in the United States have it. That's nearly as many as all the people who live in Australia. More than 5 million of those with asthma are kids.

Asthma affects people of all races. People of all ages can get it, too. Yet, for most people, asthma starts when they are children.

Unfortunately, asthma is on the rise in the United States. Each year it is the cause of 9 million doctor visits. Asthma is responsible for almost 2 million trips to hospital emergency rooms each year, too. Thousands of people are hospitalized because of asthma—some even die.

AN INTERESTING SWITCH

As children, more boys than girls have asthma. Among adults, though, more females than males have asthma.

Many people have asthma, but with the right care and medicine, they can still enjoy an active life.

Yet there is another side to the story. It's not all doom and gloom. Many famous people have done quite well despite having asthma. Four U.S. presidents have had asthma. These were Theodore Roosevelt, Woodrow Wilson, Calvin Coolidge, and John F. Kennedy. The famous classical composer Ludwig von Beethoven had asthma. So did the author Charles Dickens. There are countless others as well. Today, many people with this condition have very few attacks. They live full and active lives. If you have asthma, you can, too.

GLOSSARY

airways — the tubes that carry air in and out of your lungs

asthma — a medical condition that affects a person's breathing

asthma attack — when the inner walls of the tubes leading to the lungs greatly narrow, making it hard to breathe

contagious — refers to an illness that can be spread through direct contact with someone

dander — small scales from the skin or hair of an animal

inflamed — a condition in which the lungs' airways become hot, swollen, and reddened

inhaler — a small device that lets you inhale medicine through your mouth

irritants — anything that causes a part of the body to hurt or become sore or swollen

peak flow meter — a small device that measures how well your lungs are working

pollen — the tiny grains produced by flowering plants

symptoms — signs of an illness

triggers — things that can bring on an asthma attack

wheezing — difficult breathing that makes a whistling sound

FIND OUT MORE

BOOKS

Baldwin, Carol. *Asthma*. Chicago: Heinemann Library, 2003.

Gray, Shirley Wimbish. *Living with Asthma*. Chanhassen, MN: Child's World, 2003.

Parker, Steve. *Allergies*. Chicago: Heinemann Library, 2004.

WEB SITES

Asthma—Kids Exercise

www.lungsandiego.org/asthma/kids_exercise.asp

Visit this Web site for information on how kids with asthma can best enjoy exercise.

Just For Kids—Puzzles on Asthma

www.aaaai.org/patients/just4kids/default.stm

Go to this American Academy of Allergy Asthma & Immunology Web site and you'll find some great puzzles and word search games on asthma.

Asthma—Kids.CA

www.asthma.ca/global/kids.php

This Web site provides information about asthma, treatment, management, and living with it.

INDEX

Page numbers in **boldface** are illustrations

About the Author

Award-winning author Elaine Landau has written more than three hundred books for young readers. Many of these are on health and science topics.

Ms. Landau received her bachelor's degree in English and journalism from New York University and a master's degree in library and information science from Pratt Institute. You can visit Elaine Landau at her Web site: www.elainelandau.com.